Before My Eyes

OTHER BOOKS BY RAYMOND H. HAAN

Singing the Gamut

Word Songs and Whimsies

Alphabetical Frolic

The Unfathomable Theology of Fishing

Rambles Through the Heart

New-Found Land

Before My Eyes

Poems Parochial and Personal

RAYMOND H. HAAN

RESOURCE *Publications* • Eugene, Oregon

BEFORE MY EYES
Poems Parochial and Personal

Resource Publications
An Imprint of Wipf and Stock Publishers
199 W. 8th Ave., Suite 3
Eugene, OR 97401

www.wipfandstock.com

PAPERBACK ISBN: 979-8-3852-4860-5
HARDCOVER ISBN: 979-8-3852-4861-2
EBOOK ISBN: 979-8-3852-4862-9

VERSION NUMBER 05/02/25

I dedicate this volume to the varied and beloved persons who have given encouragement to me as I have written both words and music, foremost among them, Joseph L. Sullivan, long-time mentor and friend.

CONTENTS

Introduction | ix
Acknowledgment | x
Sunset Path | 1
March Cinquain | 2
Only Then | 3
Coming Home | 4
Virtue | 5
Lament | 6
Psithurism | 7
Flowering Crabs | 8
The Race | 9
Baker's Parable | 11
Purpose | 12
Consolation | 13
Experience | 15
Flexibility | 17
Hydration | 18
The Neckline | 19
The Choice | 20
Snowflake | 21
On the Increase | 22
The Early Bird | 24
Take Heart | 25
The Masquerade | 26
In the Nave | 27
The Last Word | 29
Beneath Flowering Crabs | 31
Method | 32

Mating Season | 34
A Gift | 35
Diseases | 36
Moonrise | 37
Morning Gift | 38
Vacant | 39
Twigs | 40
Sticks in the Mind | 42
Empty | 43
The Silent B | 44
The Elm | 45
Definition | 46
Creation's Crown | 47
Lunch Time | 48
Emblem | 49
Peace, Peace | 50
The Circuit | 51
Snowman | 52
Variety | 54
Parentage | 56
Solstice Eve | 58
Sentinel | 59
The Reason | 60
Winter Lesson | 62
Clock | 63
The Search | 64

INTRODUCTION

One morning you discover with dismay that your personal topography has acquired wrinkles. Attempting to dismiss the shock, you turn to the news—only to learn that the senator whom you trusted turned wormy. But then you happily recall that today is the day of all celestial days: the arrival of the winter solstice. So, perhaps you go for a triumphant tramp through the snow. If it were summer, of course, you would find solace by tending your flowers or walking the dog. Another time you might even delight to stroll in the rain or through the woods on a moon-white night, recalling as you go the habits and words of family members or dear friends. At any time you take joy in birds and birdhouses, squirrels and dogs, ponds and trees, worms and frogs. In short, you receive pleasure, occasional perplexity, and sometimes distress from the world before your eyes. Perhaps such times have prepared you to enjoy at least some of the poems in this book as you measure your experiences and responses with what you read.

ACKNOWLEDGMENT

As with my other publications, the poems in this volume have profited from the scrutiny, suggestions, and corrections of Kathleen J. Herrema, keen in perception, firm of opinion, and modest in appreciation. Since we have recently joined forces in matrimony, it will be interesting to see whether that happy condition will open another domain for her valuable skills of editing and correction.

SUNSET PATH

I met tonight a wise man, old and grey,
who, ambling with me down the sunset path,
one sentence uttered as we walked that way,
one sentence for the memory to keep:
> *Happy is he who keeps his dreams awake,*
> *who, in the subtle night of bustling day,*
> *will never let them nod nor fall asleep.*

MARCH CINQUAIN

Quick wind
nips restless pines,
sun frisks with pallid clouds,
shadows form and flee—skittish, all,
as life.

ONLY THEN

When fresh mornings forget their dew,
when bright noondays neglect their blue,
when orange sunsets forget their hue,
then my heart will forget loving you.
    Only, only then.

COMING HOME

He never spoke of being lonely,
never uttered a wish for companionship,
never appeared cross or crestfallen.
Yet once, only once, he pushed aside the veil.

I said, "It's late. I should be going home."

"You might as well be hung for a sheep as a lamb,"
came his proverbial response.

"But you have no need to worry," I said.
"You can come and go as you please;
you answer to no one."

His response was simple and searching:
"But don't you think it might feel good
to have someone
to come home to?"

VIRTUE

My friend often uttered this bit of drollery:

> *Sometimes a man needs to rise*
> *above his principles.*

Alas for politicians!
For that
they have no opportunity.

LAMENT

What joy-filled songs did Adam sing
to Eve in Paradise?
How did he praise her comeliness
and laud her love-filled eyes?

What echoes of his songs remained
within the groves and leas
when God Himself closed Eden's way
against their joy and ease?

Then what sad songs did Adam sing
to Eve in evenings long,
when tearfully he tuned his voice
to joys once theirs, now gone?

And did Eve sing a second part
in sweet yet mournful tones
as heart-born tears revealed her woes
and mingled with her moans?

Oh, so it is with Adam's sons,
with daughters, all, of Eve:
their happy songs soon, soon become
laments for joys they grieve.

PSITHURISM*

Lover of words, now mourn this word with me;
bemoan its long-lisping aspiration of demise.
Excised from dictionaries,
erased from conversation,
effaced from common knowledge,
it soughs and sighs to be revived.

What word in all our lexicon can so well sound
the gabbling gossip of the human tongue
or quivering whisper of fresh, breeze-bussed leaves?

So, let the blithe revival now begin,
let spring winds breathe,
and let us bathe our tongues and lathe our ears
in the delicious whisperings of
psithurism,

      psithurism,

           psithurism.

* The sound of wind whisking through leaves or of people whisper-
ing or gossiping. It is generally pronounced sith *yuh riz uhm,*
though *p*ronouncing the initial *p,* (as in the Greek letter *psi)*
offers a puff of enhancement.

FLOWERING CRABS

I

While we lay sleeping,
God was awake in the darkness,
gently, joyfully anointing every pregnant bud
with His mysterious Dew of life,
so that they stand this morning,
these eager trees,
translated and delivered into the glory of pink,
waiting to wash the air
with their uniquely piquant scent,
their sweet incense of silent praise.

II

If God so robes and beautifies each tree,
what wondrous beauty has He planned for me?
And for that deathless beauty what sweet praise
of fragrant, Dew-born incense shall *I* raise?

THE RACE

Every year the box came from California,
the impatiently-awaited box of gifts for all five of us.
I cannot recall what came for Dad and Mom
besides fancy boxes of dates
and jars of jam from Knott's Berry Farm.
For us three boys there might be clothes,
but usually the box contained a toy for each of us.

We loved Aunt Mimi and Uncle Ed,
so far distant from Chicago.
Aways affable and relaxed,
Uncle Ed wheezed out funny songs and stories;
but we especially loved Aunt Mimi
because we knew the box, the presents, came from her.

I have wondered:
would we have loved her as much
without the presents?

Aunt Mimi is gone now,
and her final gift to me,
this ancient, loud-ticking heirloom clock,
recalls her loving, generous heart.

Of course, I value the clock,
but the memory of that generous heart
is by far a richer, happier thing.

Going through the catalogue
of people that I love, I ask the same question:
how much would I love them without their gifts
of time and help and patient understanding?

And what about God?
Do I love Him more for His gifts to me
than for the glory of His being,
the marvel of His love?

In the race to outrun selfishness
it seems all are losers.

BAKER'S PARABLE

The loaf comes warm from the oven,
enticing in aroma, delicious to taste—
the very emblem of domestic joy.
But its lifespan is brief:
its fragrance wanes, its flavor fades,
and staleness stifles all delight.
At length blue mold infests and spreads—
the very image of domestic grief.
And that brings craving for a deathless bread,
bread ever fresh and able to incite—
in those blessed to ingest it—pure delight.

PURPOSE

The duckling peeps and paddles about the pond,
incessant in distress with cries for Momma.
The full-moon man comes down,
his bright face alighting smooth on the black water.
Brilliantly he floats,
yet being old and slow of movement, he gives no help.

Overhead a roosting robin cries,
"Beware, webbed little one, beware!
I cannot swim; I cannot help—
except to say beware the toothy bass,
for he'll
come near,
I fear,
to help—
to help himself."

As the peeping persists,
you attempt a stoic consolation:
"Well, that's the way of nature;
it hurts, but nothing can be done to help."

Then you pause to wonder:

"Beyond such sadness does some good extend
that blindness thwarts us now to apprehend?"

CONSOLATION

Walking out to get the mail
and thinking still of you,
I noted two boxelder bugs,
coupling on a hard grey place:
the incline of the mailbox face.
Quiet they lay and still, as if in sleep
or maybe in love's dream.

Gently, discretely,
I opened and closed the box
not disrupting their intimate time.
I stood for a moment,
marveling at their wonderful instinct,
speculating about the course of their amours,
and wondering what led them to select that vertical incline
for their languorous intimacy.

Maybe, I concluded,
maybe they were simply expecting the mail man—as I was.
Maybe they were dreaming of a distant honeymoon,
unwittingly provided by the United States Postal Service—
a honeymoon, perhaps in Kalamazoo or Timbuktu.

Returning with the usual handful of useless mail,
I think about bugs and dreams—and you and me.
For, like languid bugs, we incline to dream
as we covet an impossible honeymoon,
peaceful, maybe far away.
Yes, we dream—but hold a secret sense,
a consolation,
that mental honeymoons,
the honeymoons of reveries and dreams
(like Keats'* sweet melodies),
are sweeter far than any bound by bland reality.

* "Ode on a Grecian Urn," John Keats (1795—1821)

EXPERIENCE

Pine Rest Central Kitchen, 1950's

He doddered in from the searching August sun,
found his broom and mop,
and began to shuffle about the steamy central kitchen,
vaguely applying his tools to the needy brown floor tiles.

Slowly John moved in the steamy heat;
random was his swabbing with the mop.
He paused and leaned against a gleaming steel table.
He needed a shave, a handkerchief,
a bath, and a change of clothes.
Remnants of breakfast clung to his bibbed overalls,
and his shoes flopped, half tied.
Old he was, inarticulate, and mostly out of focus,
needing more care than the institution seemed to provide.

Clearly the kitchen was more needful to him
than he was to the kitchen—
and he would likely raise the eyebrow of the health inspector.
Things were not exactly right.

Pausing against a shining table,
sweat ringing his grey-stubbled face,
he mumbled his single jewel of wisdom,
the product of mature observation:
"It's too hot—too hot to make love."

Now, as any health inspector would agree,
in that he was exactly right.

FLEXIBILITY

Before the sweeping wind
must bend the sturdy tree.

The muscled monkey's tail
flaunts flexibility.

The fearsome octopus
hides strength in pliancy.

Likewise strong love must bend
if strong that love would be.

HYDRATION

A Lesson in Faith

The neighbor plies his garden hose
for thirsty plants that sip and grow
from day to day. As summer flows
they grace the yard before his house
in brilliant plots and blithesome rows.
But as I walk old Fido past,
he tugs me on to where he knows
the red, inviting hydrant stands.
Then, on its redness he bestows
with eager aim his daily shower
of liquid power. I must suppose
he sprays in faith: he looks not back,
for in his mind the hydrant grows.

THE NECKLINE

A Linguistic Observation

Pity the neckline.
Prevented by common language
from ascending or arising,
from plummeting or falling,
dipping or diving,
it is endowed with one bare verb,
with one ever-present participle.
This needful and notable article of dress
is capable, it seems, only of *plunging*

And what, we ask, might that disclose?
Well, only this, we must suppose:
(dismissing rank depravity)
the gravity of gravity.

THE CHOICE

The adage says,
"Love conquers all."
So, the choice for
pain or joy is
profoundly simple.

SNOWFLAKE

A lone snowflake drifts
on insistent winds, seeking
a soft place to die.

ON THE INCREASE

A birthday thought

Birthdays come and
flee away;
wrinkles come but
always stay.

Like a wrinkle,
I've been here
to watch your decades
disappear.

Like a second
wrinkle, you
have watched my inching
aging, too.

When your birthday
comes—or mine,
I'm grateful that
our lines combine.

And I'm happy
for each view
of creases old
or creases new—

as long as they
belong to you.

THE EARLY BIRD

Some Cheer for the Tardy

On new-green lawns above the spring-fresh soil
an early April bird, indeed, may jerk
a writhing worm with quick and artful work
from tunneled earth beneath a grassy space.

This early February robin, though,
must shiver on the crab tree's naked limb
and pluck its frozen apples—wrinkled, thin—
in cold north wind, beneath skies grey and grim—

which simply might suggest that, after all,
the early bird of common phrase and praise,
that bird with promptness in its core and pith—
that cherished bird is but a wispy myth.

May sages, birdly-wordly wise, agree
to modify with needful speed and glee
that erring adage, so that all may see
the tasteless fruits of undue promptitude.

TAKE HEART

(An Offer for Valentine's Day)

As you can see,
I'm swiftly wrinkling, part by part.

But (stemming from
no careful plan nor subtle art)

one part stays smooth:
no wrinkles uglify my heart.

So, keep it as
your choice, for it's my choicest part.

THE MASQUERADE

A Dirge for 2024

Thin and shallow has become the realm of politics,
thin and sterile as the cattle in Pharaoh's dream,
thin and worthless as new-printed dollars
or dollar-store toilet paper;
thin as Depression soup,
thin as addicts' excuses,
thin as traitors' lies,
thin as starvation—
without substance,
honor, hope,
or delight—
thin,
just
thin.
And this bitter thinness forms a coarse, grey pall,
smothering the bewildered, huddling human spirit,
choking sweet delight and even, sometimes, stubborn hope.

IN THE NAVE

Jim struggles into the pew and sinks hard onto the bench.
He dozes during the sermon, pulling himself up late for the last
  song—
but that matters little, for his deafness thwarts participation.
Just being here counts most.

Struggling to appear younger than ninety-five,
Al enters the row beyond Jim and converses with
two men at the other end, speaking as if out of doors in high wind.
Fellowship surpasses propriety.

Two prim widows arrive;
they sit very close together, expecting the thin spinster
who always insists on sitting between.
Companionship is comfort.

It wasn't always like this, you think.
Gone is strength and suppleness,
gone are husbands and wives,
gone, even, children and grandchildren,
gone many old friends.
No, it was not always like this.

Now a small and noisy contingent from the group home
straggles down the side aisle to the front,
one in a wheelchair, one pushing a walker, one talking loud,
one clutching his pacifier can of Coke and a towel for nuzzling and
    snuffling.
Is this what they were meant to be?

Later come the middle-aged and younger, some with children,
most appearing vigorous and healthy.
But, doubtless, *they, also, are not what they prefer to be,*
perhaps not what they were meant to be.

Into this nave, this holy ship of refuge, they walk,
weighted with visible and invisible burdens
and seeking security, healing, and forgiveness from its Pilot.
Peace they seek from their Protector, who calmed the tempest,
who came with healing in His wings, His hands, His voice—
with healing in His heart—
healing to make, someday, the aged, the feeble, and the fearful
exactly what they were meant to be.

THE LAST WORD*

July 2024

What is left to say?
Our world struggles and wars
as its leaders toy with the ingredients of calamity,
always assuming exemption from the results of their folly.
Their minions and departments of state
reek with injustice, bribery, deceit, and greed.
Satanists mock, billionaires scorn,
media stooges posture and prate,
judges wink, evildoers rejoice.

And the multitudes of pawns move on,
many oblivious, many accepting what is
as better than what could be,
not knowing, perhaps not caring,
about present perfidy and impending chaos—
or simply feeling impotent to prevent it.

So, what *is* left to say?
The good things have been clearly said,
though few have listened or even paused to hear.
Well then, what is left to hear?
Some would say, only God knows.

And so He does:
for the one thing left to hear
is His thunderous final word,
uttered by His angel and His Son.
But that last, appalling word,
that unimaginable utterance,
will also be, indeed,
His wonderous and
most welcoming
first.

John 5:25 and I Thessalonians 4:16

BENEATH FLOWERING CRABS

One thought in two versions

I

The fragile beauty of this pink canopy
reaches down with hands
invisible, insistent,
clutching fiercely at the ardent heart.

II

Fragile pink beauty
clutches with fingers unseen
the consenting heart.

METHOD

CAR SHOW FOR CHRIST
Three O'clock this Sunday at First Baptist Church

So said the yard sign.
Now, that raises concern that Saint Peter and Saint Paul
somehow missed a marketing angle.
Of course, they lacked Fords and Chevys,
but donkeys and mules bounded and abounded.
So, why did they not consider currying and brushing up
some vintage donkeys for a Donkey Show for Christ?
After all, they could likely have found
some sleek antique specimens—
maybe even the venerable 2 B. C. model
that carried Mary and Jesus to Egypt.
A bit of research might have secured
that donkey of all donkeys,
the immature but most demure Palm Sunday creature
that quietly conveyed Jesus through the shouting crowds.
And they could have included Palm Sunday memorabilia,
like garments from the multitudes
or well-preserved palm branches.
As a side show they could have held contests
for best paintings of Balaam's classic ass,

that wondrously-expressive, angel-controlled creature,
abused but noble and highly revered
in the annals of asinine transport.

What a pity that our present marketing industry
with its imaginative and aggressive methods
was unavailable to the hapless apostles.
As the advertisers might put it,
there they were, clueless in Antioch.

And yet . . .

MATING SEASON

Up and down,
round and round
far above
stable ground,

leaf to leaf,
chatter, peep,
limb to limb
lithely leap:

sq
whirl

whirling af-
ter

sq
whirl,

whirling af-
ter

sq
whirl.

A GIFT

Peace slips subtly over the pond
as orange sunset flows into gathering blue and grey.

A robin's last stuttering
bursts from the ring of trees
that surrounds the quiet level of the water,
and from the deeper wood a second robin echoes its good-night.

Somewhere in the shore-circling weeds
a bullfrog belches out his final burst of praise.
The cool of evening gathers gently over shore and water;
light wanes, the wind is gone.

Now the water-hiss of mallards
alighting swiftly on the pond breaks the fragile quiet.
The pair carves two smooth wedges as they paddle away
over the brown-green surface into deepening dusk.

A pond is for plants and insects, turtles, frogs, and fish,
for muskrats, herons, ducks, and geese.
But more than that, far more than that,
a pond is for uncommon peace.

DISEASES

you have without having a disease

The medics have discovered new diseases,
like *pre-diabetes*
(which you get if your blood is a bit too sweet)
and *pre-cancer*
(which you can get by showing up for the appointment)
and *pre-hypertension*
(which you can get by relaxing too long with your pretzels or
   drinks).

Soon undertakers will likely profit from a similar invention:
pre-death
(which you get by being born).

MOONRISE

One ivory eyelash
curves lucent over waves of
softly-fleeting rose.

MORNING GIFT

I sit in the white kitchen,
gazing through the morning window.
Amid the enveloping green of lawn and trees
a morning gift appears.

A rare gift it is, a gift of plum leaves,
purple-red, hanging moist from bending boughs,
each leaf almost transparent in the early sun,
each regal leaf sparkling at its tip
with one shining silver drop of dew.

The busy sparrow pauses atop her house
to rest from feeding—
pauses, surely, to take joy with me
in the glistening riches of our tree.

VACANT

This morning I gathered from the ground
under the quiet birdhouse a heap of sparrow feathers,
a jumbled heap of white and grey fluff,
with bits of string, long grass, and tiny twigs.
Something in the night, it seems, brought ruin
to the sparrow family in the waving plum tree.
Throughout past days their house
has been a place of birdly busyness—
nest-building, mating, feeding—and singing.
But today no sparrows come and go,
no chirping cheers the summer air.

I look now through the window at the empty house.
Its small, dark hole stares back at me,
repulsing my eyes and my senses.
Yesterday it gave entrance to safety and snugness;
last night it became the open portal to carnage.
I push away visions of midnight terror
by marauding beak or clutching claw,
and I ignore the urge to ponder truths or lessons.

Another busy pair will come in time,
will bring completeness to the lonesome tree,
will fill its purple leaves again with praise
and offer sweet distraction or delight
in times contented or on restless days.

TWIGS

The hole above the tiny birdhouse peg
is the size of a fifty-cent piece,
just large enough to admit a sparrow or a wren.

Mrs. Wren's present passion
is to perfect the nest begun within the house
by Mr. Wren, whose busy beak and wings
carried away debris of sparrows, now departed,
and fashioned a new but deficient nest.

So, Mrs. Wren goes and comes with twig after twig,
alighting on the small peg and quickly disappearing
through the hole into the darkness of the house.

But now she comes with a twig in her beak
twice her body's length,
a worthy twig, one she hopes will find
a welcome place in her design.

Alas! the twig's great length
causes her to twiddle and twist,
to thrust and thrust again with no success.

The twig falls from her beak;
down she flies, retrieves it,
and begins once more the comic-heroic feat.
Then, she somehow gets the right grip
at the right length, and the twig disappears
instantly, marvelously, into the house.

Now, wrens are not alone in struggles with twigs.
Our mental nests crave comfort and order,
and that sometimes requires house cleaning or fresh materials.
Coaxing twigs in (or dragging out the old) can be troublesome and
    clumsy;
but when the right twig comes
and you work it through the smallness of your mental door—
when it matches perfectly the framework and the fixtures of your
    mind—
that twig gives joy.

STICKS IN THE MIND

The house wren finds twigs
and skillfully rigs
a nest in her house in the tree.

Some sticks that she tries
seem wrong in their size:
too long, far too long to thrust in.

Yet she works to win—
and the stick goes in
(but how will it ever get out?)

The nests of our minds
hold sticks of all kinds,
the short and long, the thick and thin.

And getting some out
without any doubt
is as hard as getting some in.

EMPTY

Two Birdhouse Poems

I

Kindly wind has turned
the birdhouse face to the branch,
hiding its sorrow.

II

Above the thin peg nose
its one dark eye
exudes a grassy tear;
a straight and level jaw
clamps firm against
bleak months of loneliness.

THE SILENT B

Some act and think (till comes their sorrow),
as though their days had no tombmorrow.

THE ELM

Four days it took,
four days of sweating labor
with rasping saws and ropes,
with bucket lift and chipper,
to dismantle our aged and leaf-naked American elm,
a tree for all its splendid height and girth
humiliated and destroyed by tiny insects,
working in darkness under its bark,
interrupting the flow of its nutrients,
transforming the once noble and verdant giant
into a towering spectacle of impotent undress.

But now it is over. The final indignity of dismantling
has robbed the landscape of its aged monarch.
Now the brutality of the thundering chipper
has devoured its spreading arms and branching tracery,
now its massive trunk has succumbed to the searing agony of saws,
and busy machines are carrying away its severed parts—
carrying away torn memories of long-trailing years.

One year only have I known this tree,
and yet, how strangely deep its roots hold in my soil.
For with its going some part of me grows empty,
empty as the space that long and graciously it ruled.

DEFINITION

Two squirrels
in the capacious and impassive
crotch of the old wild cherry tree
make vigorous
and protracted love,
as it is called
(if the constituents of love-making
are nasal inspection, struggle,
rejection, coercion, and—ultimately—
uncooperative intimacy).
One wonders
about "love-making":
whether the *Unexpurgated Lexicon of Squirrel*
would define the elusive term
just as our Oxfords and the Websters do.

CREATION'S CROWN

Rain has come at last,
a day-long lathing of the grateful grass and trees and fields.
It has summoned from dirt and darkness
colonies of thin, red worms.
Under glum skies they languish in small puddles
or slowly slide across the moist and shining asphalt,
seeming either lost or liberated, confused or content.
I step carefully to preserve them as I go.

Science does not precisely know
why they migrate from the dryness of their soil
to soggy lawns and puddled pavements,
so, I can only wonder at their presence
and puzzle at their purpose.
If they form a metaphor, that, too, is yet unclear.
Perhaps in their shining smallness,
in their writhing travel,
these denizens of darkness have come to show that I—
a creature of spreading foot and crushing weight,
a creature towering in the light above them
with gifts of sight and speech and brain—
that I must learn from worms respect for mystery,
must learn humility that suits creation and creation's crown.

LUNCH TIME

You take the boiled egg from the refrigerator
and you begin to peel it.
The egg emits hydrogen sulfide,
which is to say that it is guilty of a social indiscretion,
which is to say it passes repugnant gas in distressing amount.
You look about quickly,
hoping that no one will come into the kitchen
and blame you for the olfactory outrage.
Then you do an odd thing:
you eat the stinking egg.

EMBLEM

Romans 12:12

Wind-whipped, tiny
      yellow
   blossom,
clinging to this drying,
      dying, still-fragrant
   tomato vine,
what does that north wind
teach you
      to teach me
   about hope?

PEACE, PEACE

*Thou wilt keep him in perfect peace, whose mind is
stayed on thee.*

ISAIAH 26:3

How clear it is now,
now that years have unrolled,
now, especially, that the astonishing and fearful work
of technocrats has passed from hand to hand,
from mogul to mogul,
from moguls to villains—
politicians, manipulators, and monsters drooling for power.
Yes, how clear the goal is now,
the goal of chaos unlimited.
Nothing escapes disorder:
towns and cities, thoughts and laws,
families, churches, institutions, governments,
civilization, and nature itself—
all swirling in cosmic confusion.

Yet how clear the prophet makes it,
that a mind held in holy order,
a mind fastened on the Prince of Peace,
may be itself a place of peace
in this unholy maelstrom of chaos
that swirls around us.

THE CIRCUIT

*In thankful memory of Gordon Start,
chorister, encourager, and friend*

Today a cherished listener has gone.
No more will music from my hands and feet
begin its mystic course into his heart,
no more his words bring joy in circling back.
One stroke has cut our fragile circuit short.

Now as I contemplate his welcome rest
and wonder what his ransomed spirit hears
far, far beyond the circuit of our joy,
I take my comfort and my cheer to know
that through the ceaseless orbit of eternity
together we will offer pure and perfect praise.

SNOWMAN

He stands, unmoving and unmoved.
We see his every outward part,
but nothing inward can we see—
no brain or ligament or heart.

His golden, pointed, carrot nose,
beguiling in its wondrous length,
and lidless button eyes pretend
to give his character some strength.

One sad deficiency he owns:
his frosty head displays no ears.
However urgently you speak,
he smiles assent but never hears.

His ersatz, frozen, gumdrop grin
curves green and red below his nose.
Six buttons bead his bulging front.
They decorate—but clasp no clothes,

for like the fabled emperor
he plays a foolish garment game,
content to think we fail to see
his ugly girth of sham and shame.

Though fashioned and baptized with snow,
he stands there, nameless, all the same.
Let's christen him for what he is:
let *Politician* be his name.

VARIETY

When the angel's words struck Mary's ears,
and shook her youthful mind and heart,
we do not read that her response was,
"You jest, of course."
Rather, it was, "Be it unto me according to thy word."
Not so the response of aged Sarah,
who laughed and lied within the tent.

How different their natures;
how different their faith.
Mary's faith was present and prompt,
bursting into poetic praise.
Sara's faith wavered, needing to gather strength
until at last she laughed in joy,
delighting in Isaac, the promise made flesh.

We see Mary ever earnest,
pondering, lovingly chiding, requesting, agonizing—
but never laughing.
Maybe as the Magnificat came rushing from her heart,
a smile caressed her singing lips.
Maybe.

The name of wavering, laughter-stricken Sara appears
in the Hebrews' catalogue of faith—
and now she stands in glory with sober, meditating Mary,
whose name (despite her faith)
is absent from that catalogue.

Clearly, God has no mold.
How good it is that the names
written on His hand and in His book
are not the names of colorless clones.

PARENTAGE

One wonders how often a sweet old mother in Israel
smiled up to Jesus and said,
"My! How much you resemble your mother!"
Or maybe she nudged her friend in the crowd—
"Doesn't He talk just like Mary?
And where do you think He got that gentleness?—
certainly not from a carpenter like Joseph!"
Then maybe her friend replied,
"Probably not. Now that you mention it,
I don't see anything of old Joseph in him."

Concerning resemblance,
when Philip asked Jesus to reveal His Father,
Jesus gently, sadly, chided him for his pitiful blindness
and then pointed to family resemblance:
"He that hath seen me hath seen the Father."

The lineage continues, even now,
for Jesus said that His brothers and sisters resemble Him.
If that leaves you curious about
spiritual genetics, look carefully about,
and you will see His brothers and sisters—
each one adopted, yet each resembling the Father of Jesus,

because each was mysteriously born of the Father,
born again of the same Spirit that hovered over Mary.
And each of Jesus' family members
carries inevitable family resemblance—
a cross upon the shoulder
and love within the heart.

SOLSTICE EVE

Prelude to the Happiest Day of the Solar Year

It's Solstice Eve, yes, Solstice Eve,
the herald of our sweet reprieve.
Tomorrow starts the Solar Year;
renascence now is nearly here.

Our earth will tilt by small degrees
until the ground will no more freeze.
As happy days move on to June,
our sun will shine both late and soon.

And so, rejoice, indulge in glee,
tell brooding gloom to pack and flee.
Depression doldrums fling aside;
bid them in winter's basement hide.

Good cheer! The swift, revolving spheres
move strictly through the ceaseless years,
as earth's slow tilt from pole to pole,
reverses under full control.

It's Solstice Eve, blest Solstice Eve,
the herald of our sweet reprieve.
Tomorrow starts the Solar Year;
renascence now is surely here.

SENTINEL

Alone yet not alone I walk tonight,
for the full-faced, generous moon,
sharing its own borrowed gift,
shines through leaf-bare trees
and creates for me a shadowed, faceless twin.
That distant sentinel, lone and lonesome,
searches out the invisible deer,
discovers the scuttering rabbits,
traces a tangled tapestry of branches
on glowing snow—
and silently spreads its lavish, borrowed glory
through all this holy winter solitude.

THE REASON

The wall plaque in the gift shop said,

> *Jesus*
> *is the reason*
> *for the season.*

Noting the plaque's proximity to the

Cash Register,

I was seized with
seasonable reason
to be skeptical.

But I recalled being told that
nice people should not be
skeptical about such things.
Instead, they should always think the best
about others who think
they are thinking best.

But, what, I thought,
if the thinking of others
is not best thinking at all?
Perhaps the honest,
unwritten plaque says,

> *Cash*
> *is prime*
> *at this time.*

Leaving the shop, I closed the door
with careful and unseasonable hand.
"Something," I thought, "is missing under that plaque—
something from the shopkeeper's heart,
something like *Thank you, Jesus.*"
But maybe that will come after Christmas—
after she thankfully computes the Christ-Child cash.

WINTER LESSON

The red-bellied woodpecker clings, upright,
to a small grey branch of the plum tree.
Brutal snow-driving arctic wind
ruffles his puffed-up, buff-white chest.
Steadfast, almost stationary, he clings,
shivering to warm himself,
his splendid, orange-red head scarcely moving.
Brave he is, brave he must be
to face his enemy, the cold—
life-threatening, life-defeating cold.
I could not take his place,
could not survive, though armed with overcoat
and boots and gloves and warmers for my hands.

Puffed up and numb,
he shivers on the slender branch,
clinging long in cruel wind,
shaming my insufficiency,
pushing me to covet courage
and to crave humility.

CLOCK

Tug though we might
    on time's gossamer skirts,
time flits
    (fleet, unsubstantial,
        like the ghost of a ghost)
            down its mystic passage,
dragging us behind—

    while

    this wise and ancient clock
    continues patiently
    to tick and tock—and mock.

THE SEARCH

Within myself I made the quest;
outside myself, forsaking rest,
I sought with care my errant heart—
but nowhere as I searched from start
to end found any sign or trace
of what I sought from place to place.

First looking wide, then gazing high,
my vision passed beyond the sky.
There, deep in wonder and surprise,
I read love's message in Your eyes,
and in your wounded hand of care
I found my heart, close-nestled there.

www.ingramcontent.com/pod-product-compliance
Lightning Source LLC
Chambersburg PA
CBHW060422050426
42449CB00009B/2093